Free Yourself from Anxiety and Regain Your Inner Peace:

Effective Techniques to Eliminate It from Your Life, as well as Secrets to Overcome Insomnia Caused by Anxiety.

Table of Contents

"Fear is the most difficult emotion to control. You cry sadness, you scream anger, but fear silently traps you in your heart. **Emotional psychologist - online**

Foreword

You are probably about to start reading this book because you are almost giving up on the search for your happiness. You are trapped in a pit called Generalized Anxiety Disorder (GAD). I am no stranger to that feeling; I know exactly how it feels to try to find at least a small way out of that hell. Similarly, I am entirely convinced that beyond finding a cure, you want it to be as fast as possible. And if that is your goal, I urge you to carefully analyze this definitive guide to your happiness, which is in this small book that will show innovative methodologies on how to get out of that distressing disorder. Read it! You will be surprised.

You feel that the direction of your life is approaching a disastrous end due to the constant panic attacks and what that means for you, a total nightmare. The happy moments are a thing of the past, and you are almost resigned to it, and in the worst-case scenario, thinking of ending it all: your own life. But not without first stopping for a second to read this, which you may have initially thought was another fourth-rate self-help book, but let me answer you with a resounding: no.

I firmly believe that this book you are about to read is one of the most innovative and practical guides in the world on the subject of generalized anxiety. As you read, you will learn to control and eliminate anxiety disorder from your life, and the best part: in a short period of time. In this decisive guide, you will learn a list of techniques, the most effective ones that I learned in the best mental health hospitals around the world when I was under the clutches of anxiety, and that, thanks to putting them into practice, helped me heal amazingly.

I can proudly say that I am a survivor of this damn disorder. I did not suffer from it for months; it was years of agony locked in my fears, which often brought me to the brink of suicide. Until I found a way to control it and then remove it from my life. What you are reading is not a marketing prologue; it is the reality of the methodology that I used and that you will soon know. I want to emphasize that this method is not magic that promises healing overnight: no. But it is a methodology that from the first day you try it, will make significant changes in your mental state that will be difficult for you to understand at first. But it will only be the beginning.

Therefore, I urge you to examine it as slowly as possible and carry out all the guidelines that I indicate. If I, who suffered from one of the most horrible anxiety disorders you could imagine, could achieve it thanks to these techniques, and if you use them, I am sure you can emerge victorious.

I did not write this book with the aim of making money, which is something I no longer need in this happy moment of my life. I wrote it because I desire with all my soul that many disheartened spirits who are without hope and surrendered to this monster can emerge and regain their life or at least try to be happy again. Enjoy this little guide, which is your path to your mental happiness. Your friend Simmons Graham, who suffered the hell of generalized anxiety disorder and was able to be happy again. I am happy.

If the methodology explained in this book helps you greatly, please leave me a comment to continue helping more people who suffer from this problem. Thank you so much.

Generalized anxiety

Generalized anxiety disorder is a huge public health problem in our age, more so than we might imagine, causing a wave of problems around the world. And according to the Gelh Mental Hospital, one of the best mental health centers on the planet, recently released some alarming data, where it mentions that 2 out of 10 people who suffer from this condition go to specialized centers, and that only in the United States that equates to more than 20 billion dollars of the annual health budget. And this obviously does not include the spending that is done around the world for this disorder. Without a doubt, it has become a pandemic, even the WHO classifies it as a more worrisome problem than even HIV due to the wave of suicides it has caused in recent years, in addition to the high economic cost.

Knowing that, then it is worth asking, what is generalized anxiety itself that causes so much mental anguish for the individual who suffers from it? Let's see the clinical definition according to the specialists of the Mental Hospital Gelh: It is a mental disorder in which a person is often worried or anxious for no reason about many things, mostly of a catastrophic nature, coupled with a series of symptoms that usually occurs throughout the day or part of the night.

For an individual who suffers from anxiety, it will not always be easy to find the appropriate diagnosis, because when they suffer, for example, a panic attack or symptoms of the same condition, it is normal to go to a general practitioner who, for the most part, does not have the sensitivity or the tact much less in-depth knowledge of said disease, and they regularly give erroneous diagnoses and ineffective treatments. And this is more common than you think, even presenting the entire symptom picture. Others never go for professional help due to their ignorance and lack of knowledge, and others simply because of what they will say. Or simply out of pity they believe that going for professional psychological help will be branded as weak and ridiculous or exaggerated.

As we have already seen the definition of this disorder, so exhausting that most have already heard it, but few know deeply everything that having it entails. Anxiety itself is a natural characteristic that all human beings have for our survival and helps us get out of stressful situations. But beyond helping us in dangerous situations, anxiety over prolonged periods can lead to many physiological conditions, and therefore to deteriorate our personal and work lives. That is why it is important to ask for help. Because once the anxiety passes to the second phase, the anxiety pictures, repetitive and intrusive thoughts and the terrible fear that usually appears out of nowhere. And if we do not receive treatment on time, they can become uncontrollable or new ones appear, but this time not only mental but also physiological, which often becomes almost impossible to bear, and therefore destroys our lives in all its aspects, taking away all our happiness.

Symptoms of generalized anxiety

GAD SYMPTOMS:

- Tachycardia (moderate to very intense past 160 beats per minute).
- Feeling short of breath, difficulty expanding the lungs (dyspnea).
- Derealization (feeling of perceiving your environment as a simple mirage or unreal, as if you were not in physical reality, but in a dream. It is one of the most terrible symptoms when suffering from this disorder.
- Feeling that you are outside of your own body known as depersonalization.
- Moderate to severe panic attacks.
- Unbearable fears for no apparent reason.
- Lack of concentration.
- Difficulty falling asleep: insomnia for weeks even months.
- Anguish and anxiety, to the point of scratching you and trying to kill you in extreme cases.
- Intrusive thoughts of guilt and anguish.
- Strong dizziness and tension. (pain in the neck area).
- Fear that you are going to die of a heart attack.
- Nausea and vertigo.
- Tired all day.
- Nervous colitis and abnormal gases when there are stressful situations.

- Numbness of areas of the body such as the area of the skull, jaw, legs and arms.
- Frustrations for not being able to achieve dreams due to how disabling it is to suffer from it.
- Low self-esteem and discouragement. And a long etc.

Principles to take into account of those that can trigger generalized anxiety.

Until now there is no conclusive factor that causes this disorder, rather there is a series of elements that have to do directly or indirectly, and these range from: environmental, genetic, life experiences or traumatic situations. And here I list the main ones:

- **Inherited genetic:** Physical and biological characteristics inherited by the parents, although they are not always irrefutable, are usually directly or indirectly related to the **tag** . Although recent research has shown that most are inherited by the genetic load of the mother.
- **Environmental factor :** these are situations in which we usually live our day to day, for example, in work environments where we experience constant humiliation or at school, or the simple fact of relating to negative people, personal frustrations, unsuccessful relationships or bad economic situations. .

- **Traumatic situations:** They are all those situations that we experience throughout our lives that have pushed us to our psychological and emotional limits. Such as having suffered a rape, a kidnapping or simply having been in an accident that put our lives at risk, or practically having someone sick at home. When a person spends a long time in situations like this, they usually develop anxiety disorders ranging from moderate to unbearable, and in many cases many commit suicide. In minors such as children, it is vital to monitor them when they present any symptoms, because it can affect them too much, even accompanying them for the rest of their lives. Therefore, always pay attention to what happens to your children at school because bullying can cause general anxiety.

Once you have some knowledge of what anxiety is and its main symptoms as well as the factors that usually activate it, I will leave you with the most effective set of techniques that personally helped me greatly when I experienced it firsthand. Once the techniques have been analyzed, I will go on to tell my experience of how I managed to defeat this monster forever in a short space of time with another method apart from the techniques that you will now know. I want to point out that the list of techniques that you will see below I have already tried personally, and I can assure almost one hundred percent that they give results to control anxiety. Without further ado, I leave you with the definitive guide on how to control this disorder and its horrible symptoms.

As a last assignment, it should be noted that this book never encourages not to ask for help from professionals, but on the contrary, I urge you to ask for help in specialized centers. This guide is a book from the vision of someone who was able to banish it from his life with all the method that I mention here. But it should be pointed out that perhaps 15% will not be able to achieve it, as in all methods there is always a 15% margin that does not usually work, but I am sure that 75% will benefit in one way or another.

Techniques to control anxiety

In this section you will learn about the most effective techniques that are used in different parts of the planet to control most of the symptoms of generalized anxiety. we started.

panic attacks

A panic attack is an attack that occurs suddenly and is always accompanied by an uncontrollable fear that is accompanied by excessive physiological sensations for no reason. This symptom of anxiety is one of the most horrible and can leave the sufferer practically very depressed. When you are experiencing a panic attack, you feel like you are about to lose control depending on the situation. For example, if you suddenly get rapid tachycardia, you feel an unreal fear that you are about to have a heart attack, and you feel that you will suddenly die so you hyperventilate or many times you run and scream.

According to specialists, panic attacks do not usually occur in all people, so according to them, most people will only have one in their lives, but no more. And in these kinds of people, the panic attacks will go away once the stressful situation is over. But unlike these people, the individual suffering from anxiety suffers from recurrent panic attacks and in many it becomes anxious panic disorder. It is good to point out that a panic attack does not kill anyone, but it does entail a loss in the quality of life both personally and at work. Luckily, there are methods and techniques to counteract it.

The symptoms of a panic attack usually always start gradually or suddenly without any prior warning. The ugly thing is that they always appear when you are calm or in peaceful moments. Like, for example, watching a sunset, watching a good movie or simply resting. The worst thing is that they tend to be repetitive, either twice a week or daily, leaving those who suffer from it exhausted and unable to perform normally in extracurricular activities. The best way to identify an attack is by following these characteristics below.

- A fear of losing control and being able to do something crazy from committing suicide or killing someone, although those are just unfounded ideas.
- Tachycardia (accelerated heartbeats that oscillate above 120 beats per minute and sometimes even reaching a peak of 170 beats, creating the right environment for the sensations that you are about to suffer a cardiac collapse. But it is all a product of of the same fear and hyperventilation, and that is when the characteristic tremors and dizziness occur as a result of metabolic imbalance.
- Muscle tremors being uncontrollable on certain occasions that can last up to 10 minutes and then disappear. This symptomatology creates panic in the close family circle when it is not known about it. Because watching your loved one shake uncontrollably doesn't go unnoticed.
- Chills and sweating accompanied by intense cold or heat.
- Shortness of breath, having the sensation for moments or hours of not being able to expand your lungs freely, as if you felt oppression in your chest. And this is one of the symptoms from which many people run away when they are in a closed place.
- Dizziness, dizziness
- Nausea.
- General muscular discomfort, especially in the area of

the shoulders, chest, back, vertebrae.

- Severe to moderate headache.
- You want to defecate
- Urgency or desire to defecate in the form of a trickle.
- Having the feeling that you are losing your sanity and the impetus to run away from that feeling no matter what they say.
- Sensation of heat in the chest.
- Choking sensation.

The aforementioned symptoms are, in summary, the main elements that accompany a panic attack once you have lost control of your own emotions.

It should be noted that one of the most terrifying things when you have a panic attack is the fear that they will become repetitive. When one gets used to suffering an attack every once in a while, the moment comes when we know that it will not kill us and we are aware of it before, but once it manifests itself in our minds, everything changes at those precise moments when one feels like dying, everything is clouded over. , logic does not obey. It is that only you who have experienced these horrible sensations know that it is very difficult to face it only with our mental strength to say no, nothing happens.

In the same way as anxiety, the main causes that produce a panic picture are due in a high percentage to the predisposition to suffer it or perhaps to a specific situation that causes it in your subconscious, reaching the conscious symptoms and from there everything What does it mean to have an attack? Fortunately, there are many effective techniques capable of stopping a panic attack at the time. Below you will learn some of the best techniques that personally helped me incredibly through this hell. After suffering from anxiety for 10 years and having tried numerous healing methods, in my opinion these techniques that you will learn are the best I know of in the world. I hope you put them into practice and they help you.

The technique of not breathing naturally in the attack

Once you have fallen into a panic attack we know from experience that it will not stop in 10 or 15 minutes if we do nothing, but by applying this technique we will stop it no matter what... this technique is simple, it basically consists of holding our breath as long as possible. possible... I learned this technique in Kalsubai India when I was looking for ways to help me when I did a gap year retreat, and believe me I found it. Once I learned it after practicing it for 7 days with my teacher, the panic attack occurred right in the middle of a meeting of friends in an Italian restaurant. And you know what? I executed it as I had learned it and the result was wonderful, something that had never happened to me before with so many methods... if it were to occur, they would surely do it with all the symptoms or part of those that you already read in the part above, the first action you should take regardless of muscle tremors is: with both hands cover your mouth and nose as hard as you can... even if you feel like you are dying at that moment, you know it is a panic attack, and you will not die despite the strong beating of your heart or the uncertainty and anguish of the fear of dying of anything. You should not uncover your mouth in 10, 20, 30, 40 seconds... even if you feel that you are short of breath, you should not uncover your mouth, you must continue supporting... I want to be repetitive, you should not remove your hands for at least 45 seconds. I assure you that nothing will happen to you and your panic attack and tremors will gradually disappear. If in this case the tremors are still very strong, take a deep breath and again cover your mouth and nose with your hands for another 30 seconds... once 60 or 80 seconds have passed since the fierce panic attack began, you will begin to feel like The tremors in your whole body, especially in your arms, will gradually decrease, and your anguish and fear will begin to disappear. That is due to the drop in oxygen that you inhaled and therefore it dropped in the central nervous system. By nature, the central system sends electrical impulses to the entire muscular nervous system causing them to begin to relax at the moment and logically this action produced a physiological reaction of peace and tranquility, and again returning your breathing and mental tranquility.

This technique is simple, fortunately it works in the majority of 8 out of 10 people, at least that is the percentage that is available in the mental health centers where it is used. One of the most effective techniques that there is and that most are unaware of. Remember then, you must practice it before and do it in a calm and conscious way like this. If you are not used to it, you should try to hold your breath for 20 seconds first and gradually increase until you reach 40 or 60 seconds. Inhale and exhale the air slowly... as you learn, the peace of mind that practicing it also leaves you will be incredible. A week will be enough to control your breathing and endure perhaps 60 seconds, but 40 is optimal to be effective. Believe me, I applied this at the time and the panic attack even in the middle of social gatherings disappeared.

Also remember to always carry the scent of lavender with you. It is one of the best known in the world of science as a powerful calming agent for our central nervous system capable of helping to reduce anxiety and panic attacks. Therefore, once you feel that the panic attack is starting, you should immediately spread lavender oil near your nose and neck, in this way you will begin to relax until you are completely calm in a few minutes. It is also highly recommended to consume lavender tea. Although, it should be mentioned that the specialist in panic disorders is the psychiatrist or psychologist, and you can go to them and they will be of great support in the healing process.

Crazy Laughter Technique

It basically consists of starting to laugh like you're crazy if it happens at home, if you're surrounded by people try to get out of there and do it in the bathroom. It may be hard for you to assimilate it when you read it, but you read well. Experts in mental health and cognitive therapy around the globe have started using the technique pioneered by global psychoanalyst Markus who named CRAZY LAUGHTER as a revolutionary technique with impressive results in people suffering from panic attack disorder. When a person begins to suffer from a panic attack, in a mental health center they would be asked not to be afraid and to specifically start laughing out loud, just as if they were crazy. And obviously, it is followed by the words that nothing will happen, that it is simply a panic attack... visibly they are acted laughter, but that inside our minds our central nervous system is mistaken or at least confused. This impressive and simple technique is more effective if the person who suffers from it is with someone they trust who will encourage her that nothing will happen while she laughs out loud trying to confuse her nervous system and thus decrease and stop the attack of panic.

Mental health experts found that when an individual suffered a panic attack and immediately started laughing and just focused on it, the panic attack and all its symptoms disappeared within 2 to 3.5 minutes of starting. And this resided mainly from the fact that he was diverting his attention from the physiological sensations of the problem, and as a consequence his brain, which controls the nervous system, progressively decreased the electrical impulses from the nervous system to the body, incredibly reducing discomfort. It is worth mentioning that this revolutionary technique is still under investigation, but it should be noted that personally it was one of the best I have used and it helped me incredibly. And that thousands of others are helping right now.

Those moments when I had a fierce panic attack in the middle of the night still come to my mind, and thanks to this technique I managed to control and eliminate it in a couple of minutes. And it was so easy, only in the midst of my own fear I began to laugh like crazy, yes, like crazy, and I repeated self-affirmation phrases to the subconscious, 'I couldn't beat myself, I was stronger...' that I would be happy despite those discomforts followed by many more positive phrases... although it seems absurd and stupid, it impressively disappeared... so when a panic attack comes back, don't forget it, laugh like crazy, the louder the better. Laugh and tell him that you love him, that he is not a match to beat you. Believe me, the more you do it each day you have one as time goes by it will disappear . But it should be noted that first you must learn how to laugh, and this is logically achieved by practicing... Try to laugh at that chaotic moment where fear takes over you, as if something funny is happening... I know it's very easy to say, but I did. I suffered and at the time it is difficult to put it into practice, but the first step is that: to do it, and it is a step to your victory. If you learn to laugh loud and steady, I assure you that you will not fear having a panic attack again. It's funny how this confidence-based technique beats him.

Habanero Chili Technique

It will seem incredible to you, and yes, perhaps you have not heard this technique. Although it is called in different ways in India, not all of them use the same spiciness, but par excellence it is one of the best. I must say that this technique is not the definitive solution as it is to uproot anxiety, but it does help and I can say that it is one of the most powerful at the moment, and it is simple because the spiciness causes a large amount of hormones to be released of happiness that causes the altered state of the mind and nervous system to be interrupted, causing it to return to its natural state. So this technique is super easy to do... I remember that I used it several times when I had panic attacks and it was one of my favorites because of its effectiveness. When I was having a panic attack filled with uncontrollable tremors and fears, I would chew a green habanero and immediately the spiciness of the habanero would make me break out in a sweat and feel enchilado, and then it would cause me to spit it out. The ideal is to keep it chewing for 20 seconds. Its flavor is very strong and almost impossible to resist. This stops the panic attack in a matter of minutes yes or yes, unlike the techniques above, with the itching the only side effect is to endure the spiciness in the mouth. You should not swallow it but only chew it for 20 or 30 seconds containing its extreme itching, and then rinse with water and allow its itching to dissipate, but in that time it will take effect by releasing large amounts of hormones in our brain that will soon make you calm down the panic attack... something to say, is that if you want to use it on the street or when you feel that you may have a panic attack; Chew it, but always carry a good bottle of water with you because although it can take away a panic attack quickly if you don't carry enough water, the itching is very powerful, and if you're not used to it, you'll feel horrible...

Incredible exercises against anxiety

I know that if you suffer from anxiety, the last thing you probably want is to exercise. However, let me tell you that carrying out physical activity is one of the best, if you read correctly, of the best ways to defeat this demon of generalized anxiety. Performing physical activity is scientifically endorsed and proven to prevent hundreds of chronic degenerative conditions and grant a sense of well-being and peace of mind. In addition to preventing you from going back if you have already taken a few steps, it helps you so that if they return they are with less force. But you will wonder is it true? Well, of course, yes, and then you will know why.

- Through the release of different kinds of hormones, such as endogenous, endorphins, serotonins that produce a high state of well-being throughout our mind and body. All these different hormones when exercising are released into our bloodstream producing effects similar to those of some drugs. That is, feelings of well-being, but obviously without the damage caused by drugs.

- When we exercise daily, we eliminate all those anxieties and worries that accumulate from our minds.

But knowing what the benefits are around anxiety disorders, you will ask yourself, and how long is it recommended to exercise?

Recommended time

According to a recent study carried out at the Oxford Research Institute, he carried out an experiment for 7 months with more than 1000 participants and discovered that with 20 minutes a day of quality physical activity, much of the anxious symptoms. Such as anguish, panic attacks, insomnia that tend to occur to a greater extent at night. As additional data, they suggest that for no reason should exercise be carried out as a mandatory task, but quite the contrary, it should be enjoyed as one of our daily activities, such as having breakfast, bathing, etc. And if you carry it out with that attitude, it will be much easier to go out and cope with such an annoying condition, and it will develop strength and self-confidence, likewise it will increase your pulmonary and cardiac system, making constant choking and shortness of breath due to anxiety decrease or, as in my case, disappear thanks to physical activity.

Now you know roughly the benefits of exercise now you may wonder, but is any exercise good or are there specific ones? Well, any physical activity is recommended, but according to three of the best health institutes in Canada, the USA and the United Kingdom, such as Youhealth, Manhardunite and Sumbert, they have agreed that at least 92% of the individuals studied in tests Controlled women who carried out running or low-impact walking for at least 30 to 40 minutes a day impressively reduced almost 90% of the symptoms. In second place was the sport of moderate bicycling that conferred at least 75 percent improvement, and in third place was the sport of swimming with the same huge results of 73 percent and with a noticeable mood improvement. It should be suggested that regardless of the sport you choose, the individual suffering from generalized anxiety disorder should choose the physical activity that they are really passionate about and not get carried away by this study that, although it is very complete, if it is forced, it will not obtain results... because, if it is forced, even if it is an exercise that releases the hormones of happiness, in the end the subconscious will take it as a boring and annoying task, and instead of helping it it will be the opposite: frustration and muscular discomfort.

Muscle discomfort

The overload that the anxiety disorder produces in our muscular system is very common, and it usually causes great discomfort from pain, cramps, discomfort, sensations of heat and cold, and sharp pains in our neck and shoulder area, and that in most of cases it produces severe headaches for weeks and low energy accompanied by drowsiness.

One of the best practices for the prevention and cure of these discomforts is to practice stretches every day that are exclusively derived from yoga and that are the most used by specialists, particularly for this type of condition. Because it oxygenates our entire musculoskeletal system in a matter of minutes, bringing immediate well-being to that area. If you want to learn, just browse the internet and look for techniques to relax the body with yoga. There are thousands of videos on this point that it will take you 10 minutes to make each day. I must add that something that is really good and that helps a lot are massages as a complement to any treatment you take against anxiety, because they help to release all that accumulated energy in areas such as the neck and shoulders that when moving with the massage you immediately feel relaxation and immediate well-being. Simply ask a member of your family to massage in circles in the direction and against the clock hands in the area of your upper back and neck. You can still search the internet for how to massage for anxiety and stress and you will get hundreds of videos with which you can learn a new tool that will help you overcome and control some symptoms of it.

Overcome insomnia to be able to sleep and not suffer the feeling that it is dawn

Having insomnia is one of the scariest things you can have if you add the fear of not being able to sleep. Insomnia is basically not being able to sleep, even if one is tired and wants to, one cannot fall asleep and we usually spend tossing and turning in bed with our brains very active and that is the product of the same anxiety and in many cases of being afraid of not Being able to fall asleep and look at the clock and see the hours go by and the daylight arrive... is a fear that many people have...

Insomnia is suffered by at least 67% of all those who suffer from moderate or chronic anxiety. This derived disorder, together with panic attacks and mental anguish, is one of the most frightening symptoms for those who suffer from this condition. Regardless of the main cause that generates it, 88% of insomnia is caused directly or indirectly by generalized anxiety disorder (GAD). Fortunately, there are some effective methods and techniques that we can use and therapies that we can take to get out of this disorder that in the majority becomes so frustrating and debilitating, causing suicide in at least 7 out of 100 people. So now that you have a clear idea, now I'll show you what you don't have to do before trying to sleep.

- If we suffer from this disease, we always have to go to sleep at the same time, if it is at 9, always at 9, because this is how we program our internal clock and if we do so, it will adjust naturally and therefore secrete hormones vital for us to fall asleep. So always at the same time, the best thing to do is 8:30 a maximum, 10 no more.

- Do not eat more food at night. As a specific recommendation, it is to avoid at all costs those foods and products such as: sugary foods, sweet cakes, very greasy foods, very spicy foods, sweets, which are usually very difficult to digest and logically it will be more difficult to fall asleep. because they elevate and saturate our nocturnal digestive and metabolic functioning, causing us to lose hours walking around. So watch out! You should not consume these foods after 7 pm if you have the problem.

- Adjust a mental pattern at least 15 minutes before going to bed, such affirmations or thoughts have to be positive, such as listening to your 3 favorite songs, the most relaxing you have to stimulate your sensory senses or perhaps, they can be a dozen beautiful images of relaxing landscapes that will help your subconscious to take those visual impulses and send a positive response, or through the sensations you can do meditation at least 10 minutes before going to sleep. It is one of the best habits you can do.

- Try not to sleep during the day for more than 25 minutes so that sleep doesn't escape you at night and you get more anxious.

- Leave your cell phone in another area of your house, do not take it to your room or if you do, turn it off! also never use your cell phone an hour before going to sleep.

- Try to keep your room free of annoying noise, to do so, cover as much noise as possible, windows, doors, etc. In addition to keeping your room in total darkness, which is essential so that your hypothalamus begins to release sleep hormones and you begin to perceive those sensations before sleeping.

- Fundamental, do not forget to sunbathe at least 30 minutes a day as it is very important to achieve optimal quality of restful sleep.
- Do not consume sweets two hours before because they prevent you from sleeping.

Once you start to change from habits to good habits, it's time to start fully with the technique that helped me the most in those dark moments when I couldn't sleep, and I cried because I couldn't sleep. This technique is known by different names in different health centers around the planet, but in this guide we will call it post-sleep relaxation.

✓ 35 minutes before going to sleep, you must go to your room alone. Do not forget that you have to have a comfortable chair or armchair in front of a relaxing photograph or painting, but be careful! It should not be from your cell phone or computer, you must print at least 3 color photographs and put them in your room in front of you. This landscape must be something really beautiful, I recommend harmonious landscapes that instill peace. You can attach it to the wall with glue or tape so that you can comfortably observe the landscape.

✓ Once you are comfortable and sitting with the correct posture with your back straight in front of your landscape, at that moment you have to imagine yourself making a mental image of yourself within the landscape, imagining that you exist within that world in front of you and in it you have peace of mind , while you enjoy a walk through that wonderful place, be it the sea, a beautiful afternoon or a walk through the forest... you feel that you breathe the freshness of the air and it hits your face, making you feel more serene, while all kinds of singing surrounds you. of birds are heard and adorn all that paradisiacal environment in which you are happily walking... At this point you must try with your imagination to create all the ranges of physiological sensations as if you could feel it in real. At this point, while looking at the wonderfully calm landscape in front of you...

> Once this mental exercise has been carried out for at least 20 minutes, you must close your eyes and inhale as deeply as possible that your lungs allow, and once done, keeping your eyes closed you will have to recreate the same landscape that you have just carried out, but without seeing the painting. This time everything will be in your mind... something to mention is that you should never stop breathing as slowly as possible without forcing it, but fluidly.

Once the whole scene has been carried out in your mind, you must say to yourself with a firm voice and with determined confidence: "tonight I will sleep so peacefully, full of peace after having walked through that peaceful landscape that gave me a tranquility in my soul: "I will sleep peacefully, quickly and without fear because I am happy...". Something very important is that you should not forget to repeat it for at least 10 minutes, if you do it daily this positive message will automatically draw a mental pattern in your subconscious and in some way it will obey by reprogramming a new pattern and eliminating the old one you had, and produced everything when You went to sleep and you couldn't do that when you wanted to sleep you couldn't, because your mind was active and restless with overflowing thoughts. This simple but powerful technique begins to give results in the first 10 sessions, that is, if you do it daily after 10 to 15 days you will begin to see incredible results in how your anxiety decreases...

Once you have finished saying to yourself: "tonight I will sleep like never before in my life full of peace and tranquility, what follows is to enter a state of deep relaxation with the following technique called breath cut in lapses, it basically consists of hold your breath for 13 seconds and then breathe for 13 seconds... and you will do this over a period of at least 2.5 minutes... this technique makes your nervous system send direct signals to your pineal gland causing it to produce and secrete the whole of hormones to be able to enter the phases prior to falling asleep.

When you have done exactly as I describe it here, you have to go to bed with your mind blank, that is, you do not have to accommodate those negative thoughts that you had before that you were not going to be able to sleep. You must reject all those kinds of thoughts, and just close your eyes and think about resting nothing else... I am totally convinced that if you carry it out as I expose it here, you will take a vital step in your quality of life towards the healing of your disorder.

The most effective infusions to combat insomnia caused by anxiety

Lavender tea : It is considered one of the most effective and powerful plants to reduce anxiety. And it is widely used to help fall asleep in insomnia disorders. Needless to say, they contain numerous sleep-inducing properties as well as being a powerful sleep regular. The most precise dose is an infusion 50 minutes before going to sleep, it is recommended to consume it at least 5 times a week.

Valerian tea : especially used to reduce and calm anxiety nerves. The recommended dose is 2 infusions 45 minutes before going to bed.

Passionflower tea: it is one of the most used support herbs for the treatment of insomnia symptoms, the recommended dose is 2 infusions 1 hour before going to bed.

Te de tila: this wonderful plant is one of the best teas to fall asleep thanks to its powerful sedative effect, so its properties are widely used to calm anxiety and chronic stress, in addition to helping to a great extent to be able to fall asleep quickly after an hour of consuming it. Thanks to the fact that it acts mainly at the level of our central nervous system. Likewise, its antispasmodic properties help to calm pain such as menstrual stomach cramps. The recommended dose is two sachets in an infusion with 200 ml of water. Bring to a boil and ready to be consumed. The time is one hour before going to sleep.

tea _ Rooibos: it is considered the best infusion for insomnia naturally. It is a combination that acts exclusively on our peripheral and central nervous system, helping to balance it, therefore, it helps to regulate the biological clock and to fall asleep immediately. The recommended infusion: two sachets 45 minutes before going to sleep.

Chamomile tea: home remedies have always been and will be one of the best options available to us to soothe some other condition that concerns us, especially insomnia and anxiety; the chamomile. Thanks to its powerful elements, this herb is one of the favorites and most used for anxiety. Since before it was studied in the laboratory and approved, this plant was already considered an herb with calming properties from its soft and delicious smell that naturally emits a certain tranquility and helps bring calm.

Its powerful antioxidants cause drowsiness to occur, that is why it is so recommended. If we use it together with the exercises that I already mentioned, it will do wonders for you. The most recommended way is in infusion and we can find the good stuff in almost any supermarket on the planet. It is also recommended aromatherapy products that include chamomile because its aroma instills peace and therefore lowers anxiety.

Apart from helping us stay relaxed, chamomile is a powerful ally for stomach aches and pains, as well as for good digestion, as well as being a powerful anti-inflammatory in menstrual periods. In addition to being a natural sleep regulator.

There is no specific dose for all people, but the most recommended would be two sachets of chamomile in a large cup of infusion one hour before going to sleep. The recommended thing is a cup of tea daily for periods of rest on Saturday and Sunday.

Ashwagandha Tea : It is one of the ancient Hindu infusions taken exclusively to calm stress and anxiety, added to its relaxing properties to induce sleep. An infusion 45 minutes before going to sleep is the recommended dose.

It should be noted that you can make combinations without exceeding three bags one day off for two, be careful! as long as you are healthy and do not have any cardiovascular, kidney or liver disease.

Passionflower: it is one of the best infusions because it acts exclusively on our nervous system and has sedative analgesic properties. The dose is two sachets in 250 ml of water one hour before going to sleep.

Hops tea: It is ideal to be able to fall asleep quickly. Although it is not so well known, this wonderful plant is found in some areas of Eastern Europe and has a bitter taste, but a delicious flavor. It has sedative effects on our nervous system, and quickly calms anxious, stress and muscular symptoms. The recommended dose is two sachets in 300 milliliters of water one hour before going to sleep.

1

I was able to completely heal myself from this disorder... I am 100% sure that you, being like me, can do the same: get out of that hell that perhaps has tormented you for years. I am sure that you are not reading this guide as a hobby but because you really want to be at peace. I decided to do this guide a couple of years ago to capture my experience and teach some things that helped me get out, because I wholeheartedly hope that many people who are suffering right now get ahead. And they are not wasting years of their life confined to the house or with that fear of not being able to sleep or of being anguished. I know what it is like to live it every day and also in my experience I know how to eliminate it, because besides me hundreds of people have done it in the same way as me. Being aware that since I once suffered from it, I know that now millions of people are in the abyss suffering from this disorder, and that is why I want them to do everything that I expose in this guide.

After my healing with some effective mental techniques and after thinking about it for a few weeks, I decided to tell my family that I was going to write a little book about my experience as I managed to first control anxiety and then eliminate it. At first, many of my family were surprised at how I, a special forces commander, had suffered this distressing condition, and that they only think that people with a weak character can have it, but that is far from reality.

I did it not for economic reasons, since I honestly do not need it. I wrote it with the purpose of really helping all those people who really suffer and cry this damn condition, as always a kitten disguised as a harmless monster, but at the same time that little by little destroys your life. It should be noted that with the previously mentioned techniques and guided meditation you can heal naturally from your anxiety in a matter of months, and I'm sure I'll overcome it forever.

All that stems from general anxiety and panic attacks are nothing more than a cry for help from our own subconscious mind. To be clearer, it is raising its voice so that you make a change in your life, in your behaviors and habits, and again regain balance before something unbalanced it. Something that I always like to emphasize is that if you want, as a first step, to request professional and specialized help, this book at no time encourages you not to ask for help, on the contrary.

You have to be very clear that you are not going crazy if you suffer from constant panic attacks or all the symptoms of the tag. The fact that a health specialist has diagnosed you with the disorder is in no way reduced to the fact that you will spend the rest of your life with it, but on the contrary, you must have that motivation and do the techniques that we will see later. I understand that those moments of derealization or depersonalization or night anguish can be somewhat annoying and distressing, but let me reassure you that, even though your mind thinks that you are going to die, nothing will happen to you, it will soon pass, have faith; they will pass A night you don't sleep won't kill you or a panic attack. Delve into the techniques below, which is the last step towards your inner peace.

My story of how i beat him - i felt the same pain as you

Anxiety is an altered state of our consciousness that surrounds us with anguish and fear, which prevents us from living in peace and takes away our happiness, and the worst thing is that it takes years, if not sometimes a whole life. I have known people who were in this hell their whole lives and were never happy. As Mark Phus, a psychoanalyst, said: "If you never dare to take that step to get out of anxiety, you only came into this world to feel bad experiences and not really live the life that it is." In the same way that right now you are sobbing over your suffering; I was like this before I could find the solution. That's why I reiterate: there is hope. Don't lose faith.

Some yesterdays have passed since I was in the abyss, and to this day I can proudly say that yes, even as an elite soldier I had anxiety and cried at night from fear... I say it with total acceptance, not like those people who they do not want to take that step of accepting it for fear of the opinions of family or friends and being branded as weak. But remember, it is your life, it is your happiness that is at stake.

And yes, perhaps at the time I did not fully accept it due to my military position and being judged fearful or weak. Besides, my position was at risk. I suffered all the symptoms of anxiety up to the panic attacks. Such as overflowing negative thoughts, numbness of arms, legs and half of the face, nights without being able to fall asleep, unfounded fears, a mental anguish of sin that made one think of suicide because the guilt was stratospheric, thoughts of blasphemy, existential emptiness, frustration, fear that close relatives would die, catastrophic futuristic thoughts , feeling of unreality, feeling that my body was leaving me: depersonalization, fear of dying of a heart attack due to tachycardia, etc.

Perhaps you are reading this guide because you want to help someone close to you, or you have simply taken that step to finally get out of your hell and be happy again, and that is something that deserves sincere congratulations.

What generalized anxiety does is take away your happiness and enslave you to what your fears or phobias dictate.... Perhaps, you just start or have been around for a few years and you don't want to go to those extremes or continue to suffer, in other words, easier to understand; you want to heal now Fortunately, it is something possible just as I carried it out a few years ago. You may wonder why do I say it with such certainty? Because I suffered from one of the most brutal anxieties that anyone can have and I was victorious after a few months of taking the method together that I explain here, and now I am someone full of peace and happiness, without insomnia or panic attacks. It may be something repetitive, but you must carry out exactly what I mention here, even if you think it is nonsense, because if you do it with faith: you will heal. Now I'll start from the beginning:

My hell began on December 22, 2000 during a vacation in Switzerland. Before going to Europe, I had been in some parts of the world carrying out elite special forces training, so I had had a year full of challenges, something nice in my working life... until that luxury hotel where I was staying and enjoying my break she came one day, yes. The damn anxiety.

It is well known to mental health professionals that a panic attack usually occurs when an individual is at their happiest . And I can confirm that it happened to me in the same way. As I had been saying at the beginning, I was in Geneva, Switzerland after a beautiful day of enjoying emblematic and touristic parts of the city. Late at night when I was preparing to rest because I was thinking of continuing to explore the city, it happened from one second to another; a small voice inside me activated and called me Simmons, at that moment the first thing I thought was that the food had disliked me and I was hallucinating, but because I was extremely exhausted and sleepy I thought that it was all about my imagination so I ignored it and fell asleep completely. At about 2 am I woke up and jumped out of bed with a start full of dread. I still remember when I opened my eyes in the dark, adding to the pain in my chest, it was like oppression and lack of air... a fear invaded me and I didn't know what it was, there was no logic at that moment I felt so confused and desperate that my countless military training sessions were useless. For an instant I thought I was going to die right there in that room. This was something new for me.

But it didn't end there, the worst part would come later. A sensation of brutal fear took over my mind and at times I thought I was going crazy, I was afraid that if it were true I would do something crazy and throw myself from the ninth floor where I was. At that moment I started crying and screaming, and I locked myself in the bathroom. At that moment of fear my intestines loosened and I had diarrhea while vomiting from fear. Inside the shower I spent most of the night in a fetal position covered in towels. There were times when the anguish in my mind was brutal if not unbearable. That at one point it crossed my mind to drown in the bathtub, I scratched myself and the sensation did not go away. Already at the end of the morning I realized that my own mind was afraid of itself, that was something totally unknown to me.

I, a highly decorated elite special forces commander in the world who had led countless missions around the planet and had lived through tough situations, was there crying inside a room, unable to control a simple baseless fear with no apparent cause of my own mind and that had me entrenched trembling with fear, and it was anxiety, that kitten disguised as a monster.

The next day when I opened my eyes after having slept for a couple of hours, I walked towards the windows of that luxurious room. She was still shaking, but it was almost imperceptible from all the stress and fear she had been through hours before. I still felt with my head half confused as if I was not in reality. I looked at things without their color as gray, I felt very strange, it is something only you who have lived it understand. A couple of minutes awake I decided to go back to sleep, praying that this feeling would disappear once I was fully rested, and that everything had been a product of the food I had eaten.

In the morning I didn't want to say anything to my partner who went with me about that unknown experience that I had had for fear of being labeled in a contemptuous way as a fagot or whore, as the weak are usually called in my world. The levels of the militia to which what I suffered belonged was not very tolerable, and logically not allowed. Because imagine a commander setting that example, he would be immediately dismissed. The days passed and I continued to enjoy them in Switzerland, Geneva, but in the same way every night series of symptoms of the same disorder continued to appear to a greater or lesser extent, sometimes stronger at other times differently. At a certain point, causing trauma and fear in my spirit that caused me to weaken, and logically I could not enjoy my rest as I wanted.

At home, the symptoms increased, and those scenes that immediately overwhelmed my mental strength did not stop repeating themselves, so I had no choice but to go and ask for private help. I arrived full of all kinds of baseless and paranoid fears at that specialist's office. The doctor prescribed me some pills that I have to thank because once again thanks to them I was able to sleep and the anxiety left as it had arrived. Therefore, with a little more security in me, I had a few days very well and then I stopped taking the pills because I was becoming codependent, an addict. But unfortunately, once I left them, the monster appeared again as if it were magic, but this time it was no longer the kitten; it was a monster and unleashed all the symptoms you could imagine. But somehow I continued to be stubborn and tried to minimize it with: "Simmons, you don't have anything, yours is not medication, yours is your mind, nothing will happen to you." - he repeated to me over and over again, but he said it full of fear.

According to my understanding of my mental health, I believed that these were fantasies of my mind or a product of stress and that they would not do me any harm despite how distressing and horrendous they were. So I decided not to follow the mental health doctor's treatment. For which I consciously resigned myself to the fact that I would suffer insomnia, panic attacks, diarrhea, fear, nausea and despair that made me scratch my skin and bite myself at night with obscene anguish.

Now that I look back, I realize that it was a mistake to have stopped treatment at that time because that is what professional medication is for, which somehow helps you cope with the terrible symptoms, although it is clear that they are not the solution. .

In broad strokes, everything that I have recounted transcribes in synthesis what I lived and what you now live in your experience. Now your life is hell, I know, and that is why I reiterate 100% sure, whatever type of anxiety and symptomatology derived from it that you have, you can heal yourself. Therefore , if you are going to a health professional, please do not leave him, you can continue with him and the advice that I present in this book as support.

I have to be repetitive in this and I don't want you to think that the author who writes this guide is very far from everything you are experiencing. I have lived and know every symptom of anxiety that you feel and many that you may not have felt, but at some point through the years they appear and appear. For this reason, my desire is that you follow to the letter my instructions that I expose here on how I achieved it. And in part it was thanks to the power of the positive objective-imagination method. Although I have to be honest about this, there is no magic method or treatment that can cure anxiety overnight, so if you do the whole set of tips in this book, maybe 78% of them will do well. of people who suffer from generalized anxiety disorder, but as I have always said, if it helps you at all; my goal is already achieved.

The power of our subconscious

Let's start with our subconscious. As one of the most prestigious psychoanalysts on the planet says, Frander Mrtle, who says that our brain is governed by two powerful parts, the one that governs our internal self. In simpler words, the conscious mind and the second would be our unconscious mind, which is no longer that invisible area that is always active whether we sleep or not and which is the one that is aware of all our physiological processes. To cite an example, when we are asleep, it is that unconscious part that is in charge of keeping our heart beating or all our organs working, as well as all the processes that occur every second in our body.

But its power does not end there, according to neurologists and specialists in the human brain, our conscious mind has the capacity to generate 44 bits per second, but unlike that, our powerful subconscious mind is capable of generating millions of those bits per second, so that if you analyze it is very powerful. And according to some experiments carried out, our human mind is capable of generating almost 75 thousand thoughts per day that most of us do not realize, and do you know who processes all of them? Yes, our wonderful subconscious mind. Because imagine if our conscious mind did it, that is, the inner self, we would literally go crazy.

Up to this point I have only shown data, but take a second to reflect on how wonderful we are for having that invisible part called conscious and you will wonder why? I will explain it to you simply. As you read above, our conscious mind can only do 44 bits per second while our subconscious mind does millions, even millions of biological processes per second, but the incredible thing about this is that it maintains and controls the choice and decision is our conscious mind, in simple words you. In the same way that the moon does not ask us for permission to perch every night, that happens with our unconscious, we introduce thoughts of all kinds and often negative ones without realizing it. Unfortunately our subconscious is not free, it is only willing to obey what the conscious commands. Be consciously and unconsciously. And all of them try to do as is. All those orders that you mention from the conscious to the subconscious is what ultimately shapes our entire reality. And in the same way that I will explain it to you, they would give it to you in any of the best mental health centers on the planet as therapy, because they mostly use the same methods and techniques, but sometimes with different names because they know very well that it resides there. to be able to definitively overcome generalized anxiety disorder.

Therefore, it should be noted that if we changed this accumulation of negative thoughts into positive ones and began to send them to our subconscious, we could in a short time reprogram many mental processes that are harmful to our mind, such as bad vices, harmful habits and negative thoughts, etc. Fortunately, our subconscious mind is capable of being reprogrammed as many times as we want, so you should not worry too much about your future with anxiety, because you will be able to heal.

It may sound silly right now, but your anxiety is almost entirely the product of a misguided subconscious mind. And just as you do now I did, I lived immersed in fears that even at night pulled my hair out from anguish for not being able to sleep, and I used to lose control screaming like crazy. What I want to make you understand is that you are not the only one; there are millions of people suffering the same as you, but many try and can control or eliminate it unlike those who fear or believe that there is no cure. I want you to understand that I was in the same situation as you and I made it. Yes, I point out, it was not easy, but it was not impossible either. It took me at least 4 months to control it and after a year it was already part of my past.

Maybe my explanations seemed a bit tedious and boring to you, but believe me, it was important that you know in broad strokes how our two parts of our self work and how the method of meditation is so powerful in both parts: the subconscious and the conscious to heal. quickly. As an additional piece of information, it has been clinically proven that everything we think about in our conscious is automatically transferred to our subconscious and the latter translates it as if it were something real, and for this reason it usually always sends out physiological reactions, gradually wreaking havoc on the brain. our body as nerves or anxieties.

That's why if you indirectly or directly direct harmful thoughts of hatred, resentment, envy, stress, etc. your subconscious will take them and perhaps months or years later anxieties, phobias and an unbalanced life will begin at some point.

The power of affirmations

Before showing the technique I must say that I was totally incredulous to this method that some call affirmations, but it was little, I quickly stopped being so once I felt the great results... I still went a lot to investigate similar topics and I realized a pattern in most of the guides that referred to the method, they always did so with similar ideas, but mentioning the names in a different way.

Now let's start what interests you. Perhaps you know the legendary law of attraction, very famous and with amazing results. You will question how it works, so simple; it does it with all the power of your senses, sensations and thoughts. The problem with this law is that we usually always manage to attract negative things from around us, whether they are bad behaviors or harmful thoughts learned. In understandable words, everything that happens in your life did not come from one day to the next, but you attracted it with your subconscious and then came the bad habits, bad practices caused directly or indirectly by your thoughts.

Everything goes through our controlling mind, which is conscious, to then program the subconscious, which is like our physiological regulator of our entire self. I want to point out that this is not cheap or fairytale philosophy, this has already been scientifically proven for more than a decade.

I close my eyes and see myself in the past, before my generalized anxiety started, and I can see myself with all kinds of bad habits despite my military discipline, harmful thoughts, envy, toxicity in every way, I was shit with other people, jealousy, and a long etc. And all of these together were over time directly and indirectly creating mental patterns in my unconscious until at one point the balance exploded and the monster of anxiety arrived. And that happens in all those who suffer from this disorder, many times we do not analyze ourselves and we believe that our life is normal, and that we are good people or that we are doing things well. But it's good to analyze ourselves even when we're young and don't seem to have big problems. Well, even adolescents often present anxieties due to many things, including bullying or low self-esteem.

The laws that govern the universe do not understand what is morally good or bad, but everything is governed by a law of cause and effect, and I understood it, that this was my problem; my bad thoughts of all kinds were somehow creating frustrations in me: bad character, disorders and mental imbalance that reached a point that could not hold my mind and released it causing my suffering. Once I understood everything about the powerful law of attraction, I didn't stop and changed the whole range of harmful thoughts that had entered my mind, exclaiming only positive phrases during the day when I said all day was twelve hours. And I did that every day just remember to say and try to do every action with the best attitude to get rid of all those bad mental patterns that were somehow directly related to my anxiety and thoughts that make bad habits.

In Udany Vaeru's book New Consciousness to Calm Anxiety you will be able to discover beautiful examples of this method of attraction that you can use. To cite an example, you could say: "Anguish I will make you my friend because you have already left my life, just like your panic attacks that have caused me a lot of damage, today I am happy I am very happy even though I still feel sensations in my body , I know that soon you will not feel them so I will enjoy... I love myself with all my heart , today I quit smoking, today I will stop being unfaithful, going to bars with women, I am mentally and physically healthy because I am part of the universe... all these types of positive affirmations have a direct power in our unconscious causing it to reprogram itself immediately. However, you should never ever mention negative things or thoughts or actions in the affirmation process such as: I feel terrible, I'm garbage, I have no money, I'm sick of not being able to achieve anything, my life is garbage, these thoughts scare me, etc. They should not even cross your mind because if you do it again you will be welcoming it or allowing it to block what you have been improving with the exercises, and you will not improve. So do not do it, do not think about negative things or take actions of the same because you will be welcoming the disorder, which is the only way that our subconscious mind has to release all the accumulated emotional tension that manifests in our physical organism. .

Therefore, I started the reprogramming process again as mentioned. And every morning when I woke up, the first thing I did was say positive and powerful prayers to myself out loud that they would give me and do within my peace and calm. Something fundamental that must be mentioned is that you should not repeat them like a robot once the affirmations that you will tell yourself have been established, but you must do it with faith and with all your strength that in truth those powerful sentences or phrases that you tell yourself can really do a change in your mental state, and that are effective in reprogramming your unconscious. If you're not so sure what to tell yourself, you should make at least a list of 10 powerful affirmations that you can take the first week and repeat them every morning and every night... you can do it for at least a month, but beware! You must change your habits, your lifestyle and your positive way of thinking, nothing negative, if you do, you will not need anyone else but you to defeat the monster.

Despite what was said at the top , I must be honest, this powerful method of affirmations through the well-known law of attraction, although it is extremely effective in certain people, its results are not so fast, but if you have a little Patience, which is a virtue, in the first 5 weeks of having started, you will be able to see and feel its effectiveness. Personally, it worked for me after 4 weeks, and I did it as I stopped vices and bad mental habits.... In 4 weeks I already felt security, tranquility, calm, positivity and most importantly: happiness, something that I had not felt in the last decade. This law is universal, so regardless of the time, it will always be effective. Sure, it is slower to give results, but because it is a universal law that governs life it will bring healing to your life once you have changed your old mental pattern to a new one. With the simple but powerful affirmations your life will change and the anxiety will go away almost without you realizing it. At all times from now on it begins to be positive. Yes, even if things are not good... think positive things as if they were already happening in your life as if they were already a reality. If you do, regardless of whether or not they come true, you will be sending patterns and orders to your subconscious to reprogram a better self and therefore a new state of mind free of annoying generalized anxiety disorders.

Here I show you 10 powerful affirmations that I used to do every morning and before going to bed. I recommend that you do your own, those things that you feel most identified with:

1. Simmon, today you will be happy, if very happy, why? because you can still breathe and you have many things to fight for and be happy.
2. Simmons, I will never give up, that is why I will always smile no matter the storm...
3. " Simmons no longer fears fear, on the contrary, he wants to be your friend because soon he will leave and never come back." Laugh at him so he goes away when he has a panic attack. If you laugh with courage you will see how it goes away immediately, I think that anger in those moments makes fear run away, being strong at that moment, being angry makes any panic run away...
4. No more promiscuous life, I will stay away from bars and places of vice.
5. Today I will go to the mountains to run.
6. I have goals to meet and I will gladly do them.
7. I feel very good.
8. I will sleep without any fear because I am happy without worries.
9. I don't worry about anything anymore, I live every day.
10. I'm healthy, I'm healthy, I feel good...

Meditation for anxiety

Meditation was a fundamental and essential part for me to heal definitively, but you may be wondering what this effective method consists of. The practice of meditation is where one exercises their state of mind. In practical words, it is about not transmitting any type of thought to the subconscious while it is being executed, only feeling it in that present state without taking it to the past or future. And in this state our mind, our subconscious and conscious can come into harmony and balance, and therefore calm down and stop sending unpleasant sensations to our body...

Carrying out this practice will always bring good results for all our health and much better for our mind, and this is because it significantly reduces anxiety and stress levels, which contributes to a great extent to the segregation of happiness hormones. Not only does it have benefits for anxiety, but they will be like a support when you are leaving vices and bad habits.

Mental health professionals have recommended it in recent years as an effective alternative treatment to get rid of anxiety. One of the first psychoanalysts to use it successfully and with 88% positive results was Peter Kelt in one of the best hospitals in the United States. And due to its incredible results, many specialists began to carry it out because it restructures our mind to a previous state in mental processes.

Regardless of the set of techniques mentioned in the first sections of this guide with which I helped myself and cured myself, meditation is also extremely fundamental, which I did twice a day, in the morning and before bed, giving me incredible peace . Now I am at peace and happy. The good thing about this practice is that it works almost for everyone, that is to say, according to the mental Hehl USA of 1000 people who carry it out, they witnessed that in the first 2 months 920 people achieved a 70% healing of anxiety without counting the In the rest of the months ahead, obviously it should be mentioned that many anxieties are moderate and with this practice it could leave your life while other chronic anxieties require more time, but it is a good way to heal.

Now I am going to tell you in summary how I lived my experience with this method. My anxiety was so brutal that I wasn't even able to keep my eyes closed, you know intrusive thoughts and all kinds of discomforts at night, plus nightmares and bloody panic attacks that prevented me from getting peace of mind, already in this stage of my life I was just beginning to practice affirmations. But since it was new, anxiety still barely appeared for periods of days or weeks, but fortunately at this stage I got to know meditation. I still remember that I was watching a video about the value of our lives and suddenly I understood, a whole cluster of emotions came to me there and I really realized what was happening with my life. I had two options; heal once and for all or try what he had, that although the claims were incredible it would take time. So at this point is where you should meditate, what is happening in your life? where are you? affirmations can heal you, but with meditation it is much faster.

Already at this stage I could fall asleep and keep my anxiety under control when I had a panic attack, but obviously, I was not completely cured yet, since my anxiety, as I said before, was chronic, but it had still improved incredibly from how I was. I wanted to fully heal, to get to the problem. So, despite everything and not wanting to do it, I began the search for a specialist who would help me with the method of meditation and thank God I found her. Poly my teacher who used the guided meditation method with positive imagery.

She was a specialist and used imagery meditation on all of her patients that she helped. The first thing he used to tell me was to sit comfortably on the floor, but you can still do it semi-reclining or reclining. Later with his voice accompanied by a harmonious melody I was submerging myself in a deep relaxation. Subsequently, he dictates that you focus solely on your slow but deep breathing, and then he whispers to you so that you feel every detail of how to control each area of your body while you relax it, and finally he leads you through a series of orders so that you draw in your mind by visualizing the most harmonious and peaceful place in the universe. And a few minutes later I did it, one enters a deep mental state of tranquility that is difficult to imagine if you don't experience it firsthand.

If you carry it out on your own, you will visualize yourself in the mental image that you want, full of happiness and peace... when you open your eyes again, something changes in our perception of things. Like everything calmer, slower, more positivity and energy.

I still remember when I did it for the first time. And it was kind of weird. The first 15 minutes I was sitting only trying not to move, at the moment that the sweet slow voice of my teacher guided me in the whole process of the technique. Inside me I made the mental image with difficulty for being the first time.

It must be said that at first I did not think it would help me much, but only in the first session did I experience what I had not experienced for years: peace , that peace that I never thought would come again. And obviously it had been caused by the guided visualization meditation. Only that night the insomnia did not appear. I went 4 times a week and my healing was gradually over the next few months. Many people are incredulous and think that meditation is stupid and see it as a ridiculous fad, but I can see that it really works. In addition to being scientifically proven that this method of guided meditation with images helps to balance our subconscious from the first session. In addition, it gives you great benefits beyond anxiety since it allows you to release energy accumulated in the muscles and helps oxygenate your entire body and by inertia mental well-being.

Practicing meditation daily allows you to quickly eliminate your fears, and it is easier for you to control your panic attacks than if you fail to eliminate them, if you can control them quickly.

When an individual meditates, he enters a level of consciousness similar to the energy that flows when sleeping, with the difference that in that state of meditation we leave our self, that is, our active conscious mind and that is the part where it resides. the power. That by doing this a direct communication between the conscious and the subconscious becomes possible, transcendental to direct orders to it and in this way reprogram it through positive messages derived from mental images or messages. The incredible thing about this is that our mind adapts to everything, that is, it does not matter if we have been suffering from anxiety for four decades, with the visualized guided meditation technique we can heal quickly.

To cite a practical example of how you can carry it out... if you want to get rid of a fear that makes you suffer, just close your eyes, and gradually delve into your mind to recreate that visualization with your imagination that is causing you fear and you must face that fear with faith that you are not afraid of it. Something important to mention is that you should visualize what you fear in as much detail as possible, really imagining yourself within that scene, place, thing or situation. Your subconscious will obey you to the letter every time you tell it a pattern established daily. For example: "I am no longer afraid to speak in front of people, I am no longer afraid that they think what they want. I will no longer be afraid, I see myself free from anxiety and enjoying life..." visualizations like this you should do every day. They are so simple and so powerful in your subconscious because it generates new patterns. And little by little your fear begins to disappear, this applies to anything, fear, habit... our subconscious mind will always have to obey because it is our slave, that's right, slave of the conscious mind: you.

It should be clarified that peace of mind is not always achieved in the first days, but there is always a starting point to improve and the good thing is that it is always progressive until healing is achieved. For this, it is necessary to be patient and persistent, and never ever give up. Because at some point you will. Most people who are treated with this technique achieve very good results from the first two weeks, to the point that anxiety and panic attacks disappear in many.

Most likely, you know many people who are close to you that everything goes very well for them in every way from economic, loving, social and it seems that they never have problems like the ones you suffer from; generalized anxiety or insomnia or panic disorders and that is due in large part to the fact that they unconsciously know the secret of the mind or they are simply provoking positive thoughts always to the subconscious despite having bad habits, but they are positive and it is obeying them in everything . Contrary to them, there are individuals for whom everything goes wrong in all facets and they develop disorders derived from anxiety, depression, fears, etc. And this is primarily due to the fact that they have indirectly or directly sent negative messages, habits, etc. for long periods of time. to the subconscious, such as pessimistic thoughts of poverty, hatred, envy, jealousy etc., And our subconscious is designed for it; obeying what our conscious sends directly or indirectly and reflecting your orders in your body, as well as physical and mental poverty and anxieties.

Regardless of what you have suffered or not, to get to have generalized anxiety you must keep in mind that your conscious mind, that is, you are the driver who drives the car and the one who subconsciously directs the car, and you can only direct it in any direction. what you want If you send an order, he will obey, but if you allow him to take control, it will bring you many complications such as: disorders, fears, anxieties, that is why you must take care of everything you do from thoughts, habits, behaviors.

Visualization to remove anxiety

It is a technique that really blew me away with its effectiveness, and it will bring a lot of peace of mind to your life. It is one of the most incredible techniques that exist and is known as peace paintings. And it's not that hard to execute. In fact, it is easier than you think. In a secluded place away from the noise and glances of others, you should put printed images according to what you want to achieve, for example, peace in your life. So you should place them in the places where you pass the most, because that way you will be looking at them all the time and sending that subliminal message of peace to your mind. The idea here is that you bring a burst of calm and tranquility stimuli to your conscious and subconscious mind, that is, direct stimuli of peace and harmony all the time. For example, it can be a painting where you see a completely happy couple in the middle of a wheat field, or a family enjoying themselves in the middle of a forest.

Or simply a beautiful landscape. You may think it's stupid, but believe me, the reaction is cumulative, soon in days, weeks you will see its results. Somehow, the subconscious will go throwing positive stimuli to your mind over and over again, and as a reaction it will automatically respond in positive changes throughout your body, such as mental balance, low anxiety and disappearance of disorders. And by the time you even think about it, you will already be coming out of your nightmare and you will only see it as a remote past.

This technique is vital to practice every time you go to sleep. It is recommended an hour before while the tea to your liking takes effect. You must delve into that mental image, regardless of what it is, but that it transmits peace of mind, which is what is important, and also that you analyze the same image. Trust me, it's very functional . In fact, the same publicists carry it out with incredible success. To cite an example. When you see an ad on TV or the internet and they are potato chips, it is most likely that you will end up buying them. At least 5 out of 7 who see a commercial do it. And it is because it works in the same way as the technique that I expose here. What happens is that our self, that is, our conscious transmits a signal of desire when we see the potatoes to our subconscious and this translates the impulse and sends the sensation to our organism of desire through a craving for that, and therefore you who You decide on that desire to buy them or not at last you agree.

At least 5 out of 7 do, and that's because it's hard to resist that urge to eat those potatoes. Technique works the same way. If you tell your mind every day: "I am happy, I will heal, I am happy, I will heal", but really in action, doing positive things in your life, such as improving your habits and mental patterns, and instead of staying complaining Because of your fears and anguish, you go for a walk, play sports, be happy, etc. If you carry out a restructuring in every aspect of your life, it will only be a matter of weeks for you to achieve success.

I want you to be just like the publicist who makes the advertisement and that you direct thoughts, physical habits, actions, positive attitudes of harmony, peace and tranquility to your subconscious mind, and all of this, in addition to carrying it out with thoughts, try to do it with equal images of happiness, peace harmony. It also works with all kinds of stimuli that are pleasant to you. For example, sounds of the waves, the sound of the forest, the sound of birds, or anything that is an explosion of messages of peace to your subconscious and you can reprogram it as quickly as possible and reach the desired balance, where panic attacks and anxiety disappear, just as they arrived.

If at a certain point you wonder, how long will the healing take? let me tell you honestly, that this depends a lot on how much you are willing to rigorously follow everything exposed in this book. If you carry it out with faith and patience every day, in less than 3 months, as it is, you will be much better than now. It would honestly be stupid of me to categorically state that you will heal in a week. Everything takes its process, but once you have made the first improvements; your healing will be at the corner door. There is no way back.

I made this little guide because I really want you to heal. I ask you to analyze as slowly as possible and do each step that I expose here. Analyze it! There are many truths in this book that can put your life on track if you put the most important thing on your part: hope.

I really want you to carry out each technique. Have faith... what matters is that if you try as I did at the time, you will heal naturally and you will return to what you were before when you were happy. I wish you the best, your friend Simmons Graham, a survivor who is happy thanks to the same concepts that I expose in this book. Can...